I love *Being Rock*! It w
(Katherine, creative mum of i

I saw a friend looking sad.
reflected her 'drop'. My frien
about her mum being sick and her being afraid for her.
Afterwards she thanked me for listening. I am so excited
that I have a new tool kit! (Katie, aged 15)

Being Rock is transformational. What is it to really 'be
there' for someone when they need it in a way that
doesn't sound like a greetings card? To describe that
hard-to-define and sometimes messy guts of compassion,
authenticity, and trust? Mandy pulls it off, the stories
she tells convey her hard-won life experience of failing
and learning, but still turning up to see how to be really
present. I felt a huge sense of relief: with the approach of
Rock we have permission to fail with compassion, we can
'get it right' even when we 'get it wrong'. I learnt that it's
the simple act of facing discomfort with kindness, the
turning towards, and offering to be the rock in another's
storm that is really powerful. (Philippe, teacher)

Highly recommended! *Being Rock* is insightful and
thoughtful and at the same time fun. It has touched me
in ways I'd not expected. (Antonia, homeopath)

I learnt a lot from *Being Rock*. My biggest take-out, as
someone who tends to leap straight to 'solve' mode, was
to 'rock, before you role' – i.e. just 'be there' for someone,
before trying to help in any practical way. Recently, I
found myself helping a friend come to terms with the
emotional and practical impact of her mother dying
suddenly. At the end of a week supporting her, she
literally said, 'Thank you for being my rock'. (Jon,
joyfully retired FTSE Top 20 brand director)

I think the philosophy of *Being Rock* is so much needed, especially as we all get older and are surrounded with worries and worried people. (Sarah, busy nana to three)

I laughed at your Rock gremlins – how often have I done those things, always thinking I'm being kind and helpful! I'm setting out from now on to listen more. (Jess, working mum)

Reading this triggered so many thoughts and memories about the things I used to do, and I know people valued of me. Your book gave me some great ideas on how to renew the listening me. Thank you. (Claire, research nurse)

being rock.

Dear Tiffany.

Amazing 'rock' to so many. Thank you!

love Judith xx

for my Mum and Dad – my Rocks –
now just on a different shore

being rock.

redefining listening
so we all feel heard

mandy preece

www.mandypreece.uk

First edition published in the United Kingdom 2020.

A catalogue record for this book is available from the British Library.

ISBN e-book: 978-0-9928483-1-6
ISBN paperback: 978-0-9928483-2-3

contents.

This is a call to the observers,

the people who see,

the people who feel,

the empaths,

the listeners,

the quiet people who hear and the extroverts who value silence,

to those who know pain, depression, grief, and the agony of being different,

to those who know joy and abundance and how to share it,

to those who can uplift and inspire, to those who can sit in the dark places with others,

to those who are not afraid to say, 'That's tough'.

This is a call to be Rock and make everyone's world a better place.

foreword. by Clara Apollo

'Yes, everyone needs this in their lives!'

Being Rock is a call-out for us to rediscover our art of true listening and allow the medicine of being heard resonate.

'Rocking' is about being present for someone and giving space for silence as well as speaking. It is taking a step back and enabling someone to expand and express thoughts and feelings or just being quiet with their feelings. When we pay attention and hear how it really is for people – this is a true interaction.

Mandy creates a loving energy throughout her exploration of how we feel heard; her observations are authentically honest and easy to relate to. I love that *Being Rock* grew out of Mandy listening to people who were reflecting on their lives and sharing things that they may never have been able to share before – it is so poignant that it touched my heart deeply and made me think:

'We shouldn't be getting to the end of our lives and still have so much to say which has been unheard'!

The book has made me look afresh at how I am – and have been – a Rock for others. I kept thinking 'I do that', like when I'd empathise with patients during my time as a nurse, or with reiki clients, or when my qigong students come to me for assistance, advice and lean-ins. But *Being Rock* also caused me to reflect on some of my responses when I listen, such as my habit of jumping in, which I think came from being with a partner who rarely let me get a word in edge ways …

Being a Rock goes both ways: hearing others and honouring our own longing to be heard. We need to know where to go for our own 'Rocking' as well as how to embrace self-care so that we can become a Rock for ourselves. It is beautiful and so needed.

Clara Apollo is one of the UK's leading Qigong/Chi Kung teachers, creative director of Conscious Living Events UK and Chi Time Radio presenter.

www.claraapollo.com

preface.

I am walking on part of the Dorset coastal path. It's a busy weekend. A lady walking behind me shouts ahead to her grandchildren and then apologises for shouting in my ear and being an over-attentive grandmother. The conversation went like this:

I responded with a smile and said, 'No worries, I'd love my mum to still be here, shouting and being over-attentive to my son.'

She said, 'Oh you have lost someone. My husband died 20 months ago.'

This is the moment... the opportunity to make a real difference ...

I said, 'Oh, only 20 months?'

She unburdened. For over 10 minutes I stood and listened while she told me of her grief, how she felt, and how she was trying to cope. We kind of blocked the path but people walked around us and, as her grandchildren played safely nearby, she shared. I was the one who had the honour of listening: to share those precious, private, and intimate moments with her. And then suddenly she had shared enough. She shook herself, checked on the children, and then laughed. 'Gosh,' she said. 'I needed that. Thank you.'

She walked ahead. I watched her leave and waited for my family on the path. Hubby said, 'What kept you?'

I smile.

'Oh, I just had the honour of being Rock for someone.'

about me.

Rock … for everyone every day

Hello, I'm Mandy: mum, communication coach, and lover of long walks and coffee shops. I used to be a legal editor until the death of my parents and a dear friend transported me into supporting others at the end of their lives. I trained as a soul midwife (holistic end-of-life companion) and began sitting with terminally ill patients and their families. I listened to their life stories, their fears, their joys, and their regrets. I heard their love as well as their pain. I began researching listening skills and embarked on listening training – but it was the patients who taught me how to support them, what worked and what didn't. They taught me the gift of presence. They showed me the value of 'being alongside'. They exposed what's at the core of 'being there'. I thought it was 'listening' but actually, it's much deeper than that. It is this simple truth:

Be with someone so they feel heard.

I began to teach volunteers the insights I'd gained so they could discover the joys of being alongside people while they shared their deep fears, worries, and frustrations. That was my working life – but then the lessons I learnt at the bedside began to infiltrate my personal life. I realised that being 'Rock' for someone wasn't just for people at the end of life – it's for everyone! It's for all of us, day-to-day, allowing each other to feel heard and supported.

Let me say straight up that I'm not a perfect listener. Often, I get it wrong – especially as a mum. But the patients I sit with have taught me a profound truth:

People aren't looking for perfection; they're looking for connection.

This book is a call to that part within all of us that knows how to be alongside someone. It also offers suggestions in answering that call.

It is written by an ordinary person for everyone, every day. Like so many, I have known illness and depression (as a child, a young adult, and as a parent). I've known loss and mind-numbing, gut-wrenching grief. I've experienced addiction and the journey within it and away from it. I know what it's like to sit between a rock and a hard place and not know which way to turn. I know why I need to be heard by others, but also by myself.

I know the power of being Rock.

However, please note that this book is not intended to replace expert support when needed for an emotional or mental health crisis. (Please reach out for help if you need it – there are Helplines listed at the back of the book.) Instead, this is a call, in these challenging times, for all of us to be there for those around us: to do our best to listen and support others, so we all feel heard.

be 'Rock' and make everyone's world a
better place

introduction.

So, what is Rock? Why do we need it? Who can do it and when?

what?

Ever been in the situation when a friend suddenly throws a statement at you, such as:

- 'I slept with my mate's wife.'
- 'I think I'm gay.'
- 'I'm an alcoholic.'
- 'My mum's dying.'

And your brain goes, 'Oh c**p, I haven't a clue what to say'. Turns out, there is a way to respond … the simple act of being Rock.

> I could laugh, cry, speak, or be silent and still he listened.

So, what is it? Well, it's being there for someone. Not the insincere, sentimental, or even soppy 'being there' but the real thing: being present; being alongside; listening so someone feels heard. Sounds simple? It is and it isn't! I discovered my 'beingness' took practice.

Together we are going to explore the skills we need and what works and what often doesn't. We will also look at the importance of 'Rocking' ourselves: to ensure that we are the supported as well as the supporters. I'll share some tips on self-care that have helped me along the way.

who?

Who can Rock? We can...

We all have the potential to offer connection to those around us. Of course, there are times when someone might need an expert: a counsellor or psychotherapist (and I truly know how such professional care can turn things around). When it comes to people in extreme distress or at risk of suicide, effective crisis services and access to professional support are utterly essential. But so too is preventing someone from reaching a crisis in the first place. I firmly believe that we should never underestimate the gift of being alongside those who need us in the moment: to enable someone to feel that they matter.

why?

Listening means you are worthy of my attention and the feelings you are expressing are worthy of my focus.

We've all heard of reports of mental health problems such as depression, anxiety, and addictions (especially in children and young people) being on the increase. It has been referred to as the 'silent catastrophe'. For instance, in the US, suicide is the second biggest cause of death for 10–24-year-olds.

Certainly, social media is having an impact. I've been pondering why so many of us find social media and the digital attention (the 'likes') that we receive addictive. I wonder whether it's because we are actually craving connection – desperate to be seen, heard, and witnessed. Sadly, social media interactions are simply less real, substantive, and nurturing than ones in real life. They don't involve the face-to-face connectedness of feeling known.

Sometimes we need someone to lean on. If someone else stops and listens to us, we feel acknowledged, safe, supported, validated. It's like they are saying,

'You count, you matter; your feelings are real'.

And let's face it, we could all do with being heard. Do you sometimes feel discounted, overridden, under-valued, unseen? Is this why we are all competing for attention on social media? Could it be that in our busy lives we get very little pure attention?

My worry is that we've forgotten one of our most profound gifts – the ability to make a difference – to gently, softly, and under the radar be there for others. I believe now is the time for us to reengage with the listener within us. I hope that this book will rekindle and restore you to reconnect with your inner knowledge of how to be present and support those around you. And it's a reminder:

You are enough; you can and do listen and support people all the time; you are amazing!

Let's start a (r)evolution by giving each other the attention we all deserve.

Rock is for every day, any time, always …

when?

When was the last time that someone sat down with you, totally focussed and listened to you without interrupting or telling you what to do?

And, when was the last time you did that for someone else?

When I started re-engaging with listening to people more, it began to feel like a pressure. Thinking, 'Oh,

I must fit in time to be there for so and so' became a stress rather than a joy. However, over time I've realised that Rock isn't as prescriptive as that – it's more organic. It's in the everyday moments.

I've learnt to let go of the 'agenda' of being a listener and instead to trust the process. People who really need to share something will find the right moment. The skill is more about spotting when someone really needs us, i.e. when a conversation changes from chit-chat to, *Oh, this is a Rock moment*!

'We had just finished watching Netflix and all of a sudden, I found myself sharing how I was feeling. My husband was totally there for me: he just let the words and emotions pour from me. Almost an hour later I smiled at him through my tears – I felt stronger, more in control. In sharing my feelings, I knew myself better (and loved him more).'

Turns out, listening doesn't have a time limit – it can be as long or as short as is necessary. This isn't a therapy session – it's just being there for someone in the moment. Sometimes people will need a full Rock; other times just a quick pebble. Just giving someone a moment of empathy might see them through the day. Think of the times in your life when someone made a huge difference just with a listening ear and a few words of support.

So now we know the what, who, whys, and whens … let's discover the 'how'.

be alongside

PART 1.

ROCKING OTHERS

Please listen without judgement or expectation;

without ego or need for recognition;

simply be so I feel heard.

It took me a while to work out the essentials to being alongside someone. I found it involved four aspects and that they all interlinked. In order to be a Rock, I needed to develop the skills of presence, observation, reflection, and empathy. Let's take a look ...

be someone who makes everyone feel like
somebody

1 presence.

We are all busy 'doing'. Our lives are based on roles, goals, and job descriptions. These are important. Our activities, the things we achieve each day, are central to our lives. We can quantify them and tick them off the 'to do' list. However, there are also the things we can't quantify: love and affection, the power of a smile or a quick hug for instance. Rock is one of those unquantifiable gifts to another where we can make all the difference.

> I talked a lot; you didn't tell me anything; things got clearer. (J Ellin)

One of the most liberating things I discovered as a volunteer was the sheer joy of not having an agenda or a 'doing' role. I hear people's views on faith, death, life, love, and parenting. People share their fears, joys, and wisdoms. I just sit and listen. I don't need to question them, lead the conversation, or offer solutions. I can just be.

But I discovered 'being' takes practice. Or rather, I had to find my 'beingness'. I started watching people – those who were good listeners; those who weren't. A busy hospital was a great place to observe. Why did people choose one nurse over another to confide in? What was the body language of a listener? Was there even a particular body language of a listener? How were some people able to engage with others so effortlessly?

What I discovered was that the skills of 'being' always involved two qualities: presence and silence. Let's look at presence first ...

being present

> To be heard I need your presence.

If we try to define 'presence' it would be through expressions such as 'with you', 'gently focussed', 'relaxed but attentive', 'alongside', but as I watched people I realised that 'presence' is much easier to recognise than define. And the thing that stood out the most is that it must be natural. Turns out we can't contrive our presence.

> I don't seek to be perfect; I seek to be authentic.

Rather than aiming for perfection, we must be ourselves. It was one of the biggest mistakes I made: in seeking to be the perfect listener I became less 'real'. In fact, I became a weird, over-attentive, listening lady!

I discovered there is a gift in being ourselves: it allows others to be themselves too – warts and all. If we are trying to be someone we are not, we are subliminally suggesting it's not okay to be vulnerable. And if we aren't willing to be vulnerable, how can we be a steady presence for anyone who wishes to explore their vulnerability?

> Through the honesty of her presence I could be me.

I learnt that presence involves a few special qualities:

- watchful attention to the speaker (rather than the thoughts in our head)
- relaxed physical presence (think Buddha), and
- undistracted focus.

Let's look at these in turn.

watchful attention

Have you ever been listening to someone while thinking about what to cook for dinner? Me too!

Watching our ability to be present for someone can be enlightening. Next time you're listening to a friend, become aware of your background thoughts that run like a script: 'Oh, I'm a bit uncomfortable in this chair.' 'Oh, I must remember to buy milk on the way home.' 'Wow, is that really what she thinks?' Everyday thoughts (and judgements) can intrude on our presence. My hubby admitted that when he was listening to one of our friends, he had been thinking 'I'm Rocking Anne; I must tell Mandy when I get home.' Fabulous – but for that moment he was no longer a present listener.

We will always have thoughts that come up, but to be present we have to find a way of ignoring them or rather let them just play along in the background without interrupting us. It's the letting go of our thoughts that allows us to be present for the person who is speaking.

relaxed physical presence

I seek presence not intrusion.

Presence also involves adopting the body language of a listener. It's our way of using our bodies to indicate that we are offering support. But what are the qualities of physical presence? When I started sitting with patients, I'd studied lots about active listening. So, I sat upright, didn't cross my legs, leaned slightly forward, made eye contact ... I nailed listening posture but wondered why people weren't engaging with me. Truth is, I was trying too hard. I was being 'eager puppy' listener.

relaxed

Lesson one for me was that being 'available' to listen requires my body language to be relaxed and comfortable, as well as open. If we appear safe, steady, and stable it allows someone to share, cry, or express anger and frustration. While many professional listening skills trainers advocate certain body postures (as mentioned above), in personal situations, I found that being comfortable and relaxed is much more important than worrying about whether we 'look' like a listener. We aren't going to slouch or lounge because that can make us look disinterested, but we are going to be us.

authentic

The next thing I learnt was the importance of being genuine; being authentically me. If someone chooses to talk to us, it's an honour. And they've chosen us because of who we are: so they don't want us to change into a different 'listening' person. If we try too hard or appear too earnest, our body language is then asking something of them like:

- Please talk to me I can listen.
- Look, I'm being really attentive.
- I can help.

It's just too much pressure on the speaker. I think the true gift of being Rock is that the speaker doesn't really notice us at all – that our open and relaxed body posture subliminally makes them feel safe to share.

eye contact

This was a big lesson. I, apparently, don't make a lot of eye contact with people. I can find 'visibility' hard. I especially don't make eye contact when I'm sharing my deep stuff. And guess what I discovered? I'm not the only one.

I found that any eye contact needs to be subtle and soft and definitely not intrusive.

If I'm sharing my deep stuff, I don't want someone watching me.

I guess the speaker just needs to know we are engaged, rather than feel we are watching them. My biggest breakthrough was realising that sometimes we don't need to rest our eyes upon the speaker at all. Think of all the times when you've sat next to someone on a park bench or in a car and shared a profound conversation while looking at the view and not each other. Think of the conversations which take place in the kitchen while washing up or chopping veg. It's the shared experience of presence rather than eye contact that seems to create the magic. This only works if the view/task does not encourage our brains to overly participate with it (like watching a football match or playing a video game); instead, a present experience must allow us to 'be' alongside.

touch

Think about hairdressers, tattoo artists, reflexologists, etc. People talk to them. I think touch can act like a bridge – and help us engage without having to make direct eye contact.

I had one of the most profound conversations about bullying with my young son while we did a jigsaw together. We didn't look at each other once, but we sat on the floor next to each other, bent over the jigsaw with our shoulders touching. It allowed him to feel safe and know I was 'there' for him.

Touch is not always appropriate, and we need to use our judgement and intuition. However, sometimes the gentle laying of a hand on someone's upper arm can convey so much more support than words.

be aware of you

The final presence lesson for me, has been to become very aware of my physical responses when I don't like or agree with what I hear. If I feel defensive or challenged by the words I hear, I may cross my arms, cross my legs away from the speaker, and perhaps even look ready to move away. And guess what, we all do it. Sometimes we even lean backwards or cover our mouths when we hear something that upsets us.

So, the secret is to watch that our body language doesn't reveal our negative thoughts and judgements. It's not easy. My son can read my body language like a book! Sadly, my facial expressions, and the tension in my body, can close off the opportunity for my son to feel heard before he has even started speaking to me. As I say, I am a work in progress …

Part of everyday body language is the body responses that indicate listening. They fall into two camps:

- Physical prompts: nodding, tilting our head to one side (literally giving someone our ear), or facial responses that gently mirror the speaker. But have you noticed how these can look contrived and that sometimes people are nodding but you know full well they aren't hearing you?
- Voice prompts: many people use the voice to make minimal encouragements such as 'Ah' and 'Mmm'. These small sounds can indicate listening, but do you know people who overuse them or sound like they are hurrying you along or suggest that they are bored?

I realised that body language can give us away. So, part of our Rock practice is to become the observers of ourselves as listeners. To appreciate what we do when we are listening.

undistracted focus

Let's be honest now. How many times have we all said, 'I am listening to you' while doing something else that actually has most of our attention? We might be hearing their words, but they haven't got our focus. (And, unfortunately, we do it most to those we are closest to.)

The biggest focus grabber these days is often our mobile phones (or any other screen for that matter). We know that screens hinder personal face-to-face connection, but they are so addictive we can get lost in them. But if those around us are going to be heard, we have to remind ourselves that they also need our present attention. And if we can't be present right then, we have to say so. Can we be honest enough to say, 'I can't hear you fully right now' rather than pretend we are actually listening?

Could it be that one minute of full attention is worth a million moments of semi-focus?

Sometimes, I find people need support at times when it's really hard to keep focus – the college canteen, the office, school pick up, the local pub. But I've realised that if someone chooses to share their deep feelings in a public situation, they must be really struggling, and our gift is to give them as much focussed attention as we are able.

'A friend I was confiding with in the pub suddenly turned away and said hello to someone else. I was devastated. I felt so small, so lost. It was like he said – you don't count. In hindsight, I realise it wasn't the best time to share, but I was so terribly low I just needed a friend ...' (Mya)

silence

The word 'silent' contains the same letters as the word 'listen'.

Turns out there is another secret to 'being': the gift of silence. I don't mean that I never say anything when I'm listening to someone; just that I've become okay with allowing silence and trusting it.

If you don't know what to say; take a beat.

But silence is tricky because it can feel awkward. It's easier to rush in with a response, to fill the gap – anything but the quiet, open space of silence. But I've noticed that when someone is sharing and then falls comfortably silent, the discomfort of it is felt by me not them. I began to question myself – if they want to take a beat why can't I?

I've slowly learnt never to underestimate the gift of being able to sit with someone and let them talk, to let them unburden in their own time and rhythm. But I've also discovered that I must be comfortable with silence: to trust it; relax into it; to hold it inside myself as well as outside.

The power of silence is in the space it creates.

And there's this other thing – interrupting silence can break someone's thought process. I don't know about you, but if I'm talking something through and

I stop speaking, it's hardly ever because I've run out of things to say, but rather that I'm just processing my feelings so I can share them more deeply. And, what happens when someone interrupts my thought process? Yeah, I lose my train of thought.

Silence doesn't mean my brain has stopped working – just my mouth.

I learnt that silence might not mean that the speaker wants me to start speaking to fill the void. Also, I have to accept that it's unlikely the speaker expects me to have all the answers or indeed even wants to hear my ideas! Often people just need a sounding board – by talking to us and falling silent with us they feel safe to explore their ideas and feelings. Probably ideas and feelings they hadn't realised were there. And, such exploring can be very empowering.

So, when someone falls silent with me, I ask myself: 'Are they waiting for a response from me or are they still thinking?' I'm learning to spot the difference. And, in general, I work on the basis of:

If they aren't looking at me, they aren't looking for a response from me.

This is my new golden rule: to remember that it can be as irritating to interrupt someone's silence as it is to interrupt them when they are speaking.

Silence often enables the speaker to order and structure their words for you to understand them, particularly if the speaker is a child. But it can also help the speaker clarify their own thoughts: they hear themselves.

Listeners are amplifiers: the sound bounces back from their silent presence, so the speaker hears their own words, hears their own thoughts, and senses their own emotions.

rock recap

So, here's my personal 'presence' list:

- Be me! Authenticity = connection.
- Breathe and relax so my body looks comfortable and says, 'Hey, I can be here for you.'
- Leave my stuff and every day cares behind because I can't focus on the speaker if I'm focussed on me. I consciously try to 'pause' my inner voice and instead think: 'Rock moment!'
- Try not to worry (I'm very good at worrying) and remember that I'm enough. I can do this!
- Intend to remain present and listen. Make the commitment and stay with it. Be the person they can rely on.
- Don't do anything else! Avoid the distractions; retain the focus.

- Hold the silence if needed. Just be …

Presence and holding silence really are the qualities of being alongside. If someone has a full-on emotional outburst, breaks eye contact, cries into their hands, or falls silent, how reassuring is it for them to come back from their emotional storm and find someone still there with them: being Rock. I practice whenever I can because it takes time to become the person who is happy to just sit and listen.

> There is a voice that doesn't use words. Listen.
> (Rumi)

I guess true listening respects a person's exploration of their situation and honours the process rather than taking on the feelings of the speaker, or processing them, or trying to fix them. Perhaps it is enough to be an ear-witness and eyewitness to the speaker's narrative: the observer of a story.

This takes us nicely on to the art of observing …

to hear someone, you must also see them

2 observing.

'To observe requires you to let go of any judgements, rejections, choices, or filters in relation to what someone is saying ... to let go of you and just witness them.' (Deepak Chopra)

I can remember sobbing uncontrollably after inadvertently drowning a spider in the bath. Was I being pathetic? Truth is, my dad had died three weeks before and the loss of another life was my emotional tipping point. So now, when people are behaving over the top, I ask myself, 'Am I witnessing only a glimpse of what might really be going on for them?'

Rocks are observers – we notice when people are troubled. But I learnt something significant: it's not only body language that lets us know how someone is feeling – it's also how people speak.

Obviously, we need to know how to support people as well as observe what's going on for them. I promise we will delve deeper into that in Chapter 3. But for now, let's explore observing and it all begins with body language ...

body language

To support those around us we need to observe their body language: to not only hear their words but also watch how they are said (intonation and body gestures). Body language forms a massive part of our communication. I'm sure we've all fallen victim to someone misconstruing our text messages and social media posts which just goes to prove that words alone don't convey the feelings behind them.

Reading body language is intuitive. We learn how to do it as children and pick up on the gestures and signals people use in our language and culture. As listeners, we instinctively pick up on body language cues and we are generally very good at non-verbal communication. Here's an example of perfect body language recognition (with some epic empathy thrown in):

Me: Walking along, head down, shoulders hunched, face sad …
Friend: Hi
Me: Hello
Friend: Who's pissed in your coffee?
Me: I have
Friend (with an arm around my shoulder): Oh, I hate that – when we feel c**p and can't even blame someone else!
(Brilliant epic Rock moment. Thank you, Ditty)

Surprisingly, the face alone is not a reliable indicator of emotion. While the face may reveal the general intensity of a feeling, it doesn't always communicate exactly what the person is feeling. It's the body and physical gestures that give us the clues: what the hands and arms are doing, how someone is sitting or walking. When we observe, we need to watch the whole of the person – not just their face.

When people are feeling emotional, I've noticed that they tend to exhibit one of two types of body language. I call them inward and outward:

- Inward body language is when someone is feeling low and vulnerable or has internalised their anger. They display 'inward' body postures to protect themselves. Because they can't physically hide, the body language mirrors their desire to be invisible.
- Outward body language, on the other hand, is very visible. When someone is angry or frustrated, they demonstrate very expansive body postures: they use their body to say, 'Look at me – I'm ready for an argument.'

Let's look at these in more detail:

inward body postures

Inward is the ultimate withdrawal.

So inward is when someone is internalising their emotional response. This is what we might see:

Body: curls up, shoulders hunched, head down,

hands closed in towards the body, arms crossed to protect the body, may avoid close proximity to others or may actively seek to be held and hugged (almost burying/hiding themselves in your arms)

Face: head down, down-cast eyes (generally avoids eye contact or, if they trust you, makes 'pleading' eye contact), covering face with hands or protecting the throat with a hand, pale complexion, tears or welling up

Voice: quiet, few words or not speaking at all, or a flood of words but they are very much focussed in on how they are feeling (more on this later)

The walk: head down and fast (if people are watching – I call it the 'school run getaway') or very slow and dragging their feet (not wanting to face where they are going); shoulders hunched over.

outward body postures

Outward is a blatant emotional response.

Outward is when someone is externalising their emotional response. We might observe:

Body: tense muscles, clenched fists, tight and flushed neck, invades another's personal space, gestures from finger wagging, insulting gestures, or whole arm sweeps

Face: red or flushed cheeks or face goes white, eyes stare or squint (makes eye contact), jaw clenched, pursed lips (sneers or snarls)

Voice: loud, forthright, possibly aggressive, and use of profanity

The walk: less of a walk and more of a stride – fast, furious, and determined; exaggerated swinging of the arms. Think of someone storming out (often with a door slam) and you've got the picture.

Both of those positions (inward and outward) indicate that the speaker is struggling: the physical responses may be different, but they are still fraught. To support someone through that struggle we need to show them that we are willing to be alongside: their Rock.

Whether the speaker is low and vulnerable or angry and frustrated, our presence offers safety and compassion: to witness their vulnerability without judgement or fear. (Later we'll explore what we can also say to support someone through their emotional turmoil: see Chapter 3.)

A person's body language can be more complex than the examples above. However, I think that body language recognition is all about matching the words with the emotions expressed through body posture. I started practising observing people's body language in conversations (particularly emotional and heated ones). Coffee shops and pubs are great venues for this. Also, I began watching my own physical reactions and the reactions of the people around me, because the more we observe, the more we see. Indeed, interactions (even angry ones) can be brilliant learning sessions:

When my hubby was reading a draft of this book, he suggested a bit more detail on body language. The following morning over breakfast the conversation went like this:

Me: 'I wrote up some more on body language yesterday like you suggested. I'm really pleased you thought of that. Thanks.'

Hubby: 'I think you have to be careful you don't write too much about it. Your book isn't about body language – there are lots of books on that.'
Me: (arms up, bent at elbows, palms showing – frustration stance): 'OMG really?!' (voice exasperated)

Hubby: 'I'm just saying.' (defensive)

Me: (angry now) 'But you said to write up more on body language – that's what you told me to do!' (notice use of 'you': more on this below)
Hubby: 'Don't get angry at me!'

Luckily at this point I became the 'observer' of our conversation and burst out laughing. I said (with a smile): 'But I feel angry because you're the one who made me cross.'

hearing the words used or rather how they are said

While body language alone can indicate that someone needs support – the words they use and how they say them are also huge clues. Not everyone will state outright what is troubling them. Instead, I began to notice that people use different ways to express their problems. And the way they express themselves can very much depend on whether they are in inward or outward.

Very simply, inward is how someone feels inside whereas outward is a more obvious expression of what has happened to them.

inward words

When someone has internalised their emotions, the words used will indicate their inner feelings about whatever is wrong.

> 'I feel overwhelmed; I can't do this; everything is getting on top of me and I just can't cope.'

Notice the use of 'I' – it's how the person feels inside.

But what I began to notice is that often people in inward don't tell you directly how they feel but rather 'hide' how they are feeling or what is really bothering them in among their general conversation. I call it the 'drop'. This is where someone indicates what is really troubling them by dropping it into the conversation. The drop usually comes sandwiched between two other statements and is usually followed with a 'but'. This is a true-life example from an elderly patient:

> 'I've had lots of visitors today it's been nice. Obviously, I'm thinking I will meet my Maker soon, but the cricket is on later.'

Quite often people even change subject quickly after the drop or pick themselves up, so the effect of the drop is minimised or appears as an aside. In the above example the patient is thinking about dying (meeting God or as he put it 'his Maker') but instantly deflects from the drop by talking about cricket on television.

If it's a significant problem, usually the drop will occur more than once in the conversation. The trick is to spot the drop (it's easier to notice if they repeat it) and then mirror the word(s) they are using to express the problem. In the above example, I mirrored the word 'Maker'. We will look at the skill of reflecting a word or phrase later (see Chapter 3), but for now let's just explore how people show us that they are struggling.

Children definitely do drops too. A teacher once told me he heard a drop from a primary age child whose parents had just separated:

> 'I had a nice weekend with Daddy. Mummy wasn't there but Daddy spoilt me lots.'

The other way people tend to hide their problems is with the 'dismiss'. This is similar to the drop except that, instead of sandwiching it, the speaker will lift from the drop by dismissing the importance of what they are going through, e.g.:

> 'Work is so stressful. I have so many unread emails. But then everyone's in the same boat.'

People often share their problems and then smile and say, 'What a first world problem.' Yes, it might be a first world problem, but it's still a problem. It is real to them.

outward words

When someone is externalising their emotions, their words indicate feelings of 'You are wrong', 'They are wrong' or 'It is wrong'. For example:

- 'But you said to write up more on body language – that's what you told me to do!'
- 'They can't treat me like this. They say it's bloody company policy. They are so c**p!'
- 'It's so unfair. Everyone's being so selfish. It's not my fault.'

Notice the use of 'you', 'they', or 'it'. Outward wording is more about someone or something else being responsible for the emotion experienced.

Outward emotion is often shared as an angry outburst or full-on tirade of verbal diarrhoea: the 'rant'. Do you know a 'ranter'? It's when someone literally dumps all their pent-up feelings in a great pile at your feet. It can be hard to listen to.

I've discovered that I've become an Olympian menopausal ranter. It has taught me a lot about the experience from the inside. I feel rants are like storms – they need to build and then blow themselves out. Coming in on a rant by interrupting it or trying to stop it rarely works and is more likely to escalate the situation. Instead, let them rant. In my experience if we stay alongside someone ranting, hearing them, eventually the outburst will subside.

As I observed numerous rants, I began to notice that people end them in their own unique ways. I call it the 'return'. They will bring themselves back, usually by changing the subject, or with a shudder, a small laugh, a big sniff, a tentative smile. This ending moment is very precious – it's the moment they come back to normality. Rather than asking them to share more or stepping in and offering solutions, I find that quiet presence can support them to discover their own answers and thoughts on how to move forward. A rant can be literally letting off steam – and sometimes that's enough for them to feel better.

Here are some examples of the return:

- After a major rant, a patient in a hospice changed the subject by lifting back her bedsheets and saying, 'Anyway, how do you like my new surgical stockings?'
- My mate grabbed a tissue, blew her nose, smiled at me, and said, 'I think I'm ready for a hug now.'
- A friend burst into my room in tears because her boyfriend had dumped her. I sat and held her as she wailed for 15 minutes. Then she stopped, looked up at me and said, 'Finished! Can we go to the pub now?'

When I was writing this bit, I asked my hubby how he knows when I've finished a rant. 'I feel a little bit less scared!' he said (with a grin).

beyond words

Sometimes, particularly when someone is completely caught up in a situation or feeling totally overwhelmed, rather than expressing themselves verbally, they clam up. It can occur in both inward and outward: the body is screaming something is wrong but any attempt by us to engage with them verbally totally fails. It's us saying, 'What's the matter?' and them saying, 'NOTHING!' followed by further withdrawal or storming off. It's common for children and teenagers to respond like this but adults do it too. I think it's because they are so 'full' of whatever the problem is, they can't even begin to express it.

I used to think that 'nothing' responses were people being deliberately awkward or defensive – you know 'being a teenager'. But I now know it's not their response that's wrong – it's our questioning. We provoke the 'nothing' reply. So my first (and very much ongoing) self-improvement is when I get a 'nothing', a 'no' head shake, or a storming off, is to look at what I just said that might have initiated it.

If someone appears beyond words, rather than adding to their pressure, I just observe their body language. What's their body telling me that their voice cannot? (We will look at our supportive response in Chapter 3.)

'do you?' questions

Besides inward and outward forms of sharing, I've also observed that there is a more obvious type of communication by which someone might ask to be heard. It's when someone asks a difficult question.

For example,

- 'Do you think I have a drink problem?'
- 'Do you think I'm a bad mum?'
- 'Do you think I'm fat?'

Notice that these questions start with 'Do you'. Sometimes these questions are just seeking reassurance – please tell me that it's okay to get drunk every now and again, that most mums struggle sometimes, and please tell me I don't look overweight. But watch for the 'do yous' that get repeated on the same theme: I believe they are actually a call to be heard because the speaker needs to explore something very personal.

Perhaps, rather than looking for our opinion, 'do yous' ask for our willingness to be their Rock: to avoid the platitudes and the discomfort and listen instead. One of the most profound moments I've ever had was with an elderly gentleman who slowly began to share his truth with me – the truth that he found other men attractive. He did this through a series of 'do yous': 'Do you think the man on this CD cover is good looking?' 'Do you think the gentleman opposite us is attractive?' Over time, as I remained open to his honesty, he was able to share more.

Obviously, sometimes people ask us a question because they genuinely want our answer. However, if we avoid rushing in with a response, it might allow them the space to share first.

Rock recap

So, here's my personal 'observe' list:

- Watch the body language: are they in inward or outward?
- If they are inward, listen out for the drop.
- If they are outward, let them rant and return.
- If they are unable to express themselves (beyond words), what emotion is their body conveying?
- Be aware of repeating 'do you' questions on the same topic.

Once we've observed someone's body language and heard the words they use, how do we respond? The secret I discovered is to reflect …

be my reflection

reflect: so I can hear myself through you

3 reflecting.

So far, we've explored the significance of Presence and Observing. I learnt that these are the foundations for being alongside: enabling us to witness a story or to sit with silence. But how do we bring those skills into every day? It's unlikely that someone will come up to us and say, 'Hi, I'm having a bad day, can ya Rock me?'

So, how do we Rock our friends on the school run? Or our partners when they come home from a bad day at work? Or our children when they lose a piece of Lego? All these moments are valid for equal attention.

The secret I discovered is reflecting: reflecting emotions, reflecting words, or reflecting questions.

when they tell you what's wrong: reflecting the drop

'I had hit rock bottom. I called a friend. She listened. I talked. I told her, among other things, that I felt 'lost'. But it's when she reflected the word 'lost' I realised I'd said it before. I remember thinking 'Yep, that's exactly how I feel.' And just knowing that helped.' (Thank you Antonia – you Rock!)

I've noticed that when people are upset, they often repeat a word that shows either the crux of the problem or how that problem is making them feel. Indeed, we know that someone can literally drop their problem into the conversation.

I believe the 'drop' is code for can you hear me? And if we do hear them, if we are able to spot their drop, we need to let them know they've been heard. I do it by simply reflecting it back. I mirror the repeated word or phrase they used. What if a friend said the following?

'I like my new job but I'm constantly exhausted. Still, I'm lucky to be in work and everyone is lovely, but I just wish I wasn't so tired.'

The word to reflect would be 'tired' because it's the second 'drop' on the same theme: your friend is feeling worn out.

Turns out there is a skill to reflecting a repeated word or phrase and trust me I learnt the hard way with this. Reflecting drops involves some golden rules:

- use this skill only when really needed – overuse it and it loses its effect or they'll think you're weird or doing some technique (which of course you are but you don't want them to know!)

- listen for the word that keeps being repeated and then say it back to the speaker – once and once only
- reflect with a neutral soft intonation – almost as if you were saying 'mmm' or 'yeah'. We can't make a statement or drama out of the drop or turn it into a question. (If we add a question mark with our voice, it can sound judgemental – there's a big difference between saying 'sad' and 'sad?')
- follow your reflection with silence – just say the word or phrase and nothing more

Rocks reflect not emphasise.

The incredible power of reflecting a repeated word is that the speaker is able to 'hear' themselves through you. It works because they experience a mirror of what they are saying and feeling. I've reflected many drops and watched with awe how it enables people to unburden. People respond differently to reflection, though. For some, hearing it unlocks their need to share. For others, even though the speaker hears the reflected word, they may not verbally respond but you can tell they feel heard. Others may respond later after mulling it over. I've learnt to trust. Do you remember the 'Maker' drop? Well, this is what happened:

'I was chatting to a terminally ill patient. Every so often he would drop into the conversation that he realised he would soon be meeting his "Maker". On the third occasion, I reflected the word "Maker" back. He didn't acknowledge what I'd said but carried on chatting. When his family arrived, I got up to leave. He took my hand and said, "Can you come back tomorrow when my family aren't here? I'd like to talk to you about that Maker thing."'

I did go back and had one of the most poignant moments of my life: just from reflecting one word.

There is one final reflection no-no: I've learnt to avoid reflecting a word where the speaker is making a negative statement about themselves or something that has happened. For instance, what if a teenager falls to pieces in an exam and afterwards says:

'I fluffed it. I'm useless. I feel horrible.'

The word to reflect is 'horrible' because if we reflected 'fluffed it' or 'useless' it can sound like we are affirming their opinion of themselves and the situation. However, by reflecting 'horrible' we are simply reflecting how they feel.

when they don't tell you what's wrong (beyond words): reflect the emotion

If I have learnt one thing, it's never to utter the words 'What's the matter?'

This method is simple but so effective. Use it when someone is beyond words and seems unable to process their thoughts or tell you what's wrong. Children and young people in particular can find it hard to verbalise a problem, but their body language will be screaming that something is wrong. This technique is for when we don't know what's wrong and they aren't telling us.

Reflecting the emotion involves naming the emotion someone is presenting through their body language. We simply reflect how they appear to us, e.g. 'You look sad', 'You seem angry', 'It feels like you might be frustrated'. This enables the person to 'hear' where they are. (The great news is that this technique also teaches young children what certain feelings are actually called.)

Let's look at what normally happens:

Child: Not speaking but brimming with sadness and frustration.
Dad: 'What's the matter?'
Child: Wells up with tears but just shakes his head.
Dad: 'Oh, what's wrong?'
Child: 'Nothing.' Now looks angry as well. Looks down.

Dad: 'What is it? Can't you tell me?'
Child: Storms off shouting, 'Stop asking me questions!'

So, for this technique to work, I've learnt (to my cost) don't ask questions. If I find myself framing a question in my mind, I try to catch it before it's out of my mouth. It's a normal response, but I have come to realise that when someone is caught up in emotional turmoil, they don't even know how to begin to describe it. Questions can then become added pressure.

Let's try the scenario again:

Child: Not speaking but brimming with sadness and frustration.
Dad: 'Oh, you look sad'.
Child: Wells up with tears but just shakes his head.
Dad: Just sits as a Rock, staying present, holding the silence.
Child: 'It's just that …' The child starts to speak, and the emotion is expressed.

So, emotional reflecting involves: name the emotion and then don't say anything else. We have to hold the silence for this to work.

Oh, and I've learnt to watch my body language with this technique: to keep it gentle. Be careful not to ask questions with your eyes or make too much direct eye contact during the silence. It's about giving someone space but still being there when they come back to you.

'I came home from work and did a full-on rant in the kitchen while my husband quietly washed the dishes. When I was done, he looked up at me and grinned. "Your technique works," he said. I hadn't even noticed that he had named the emotion to me at the beginning which unlocked my rant. All he had said was, "You don't look too happy." And then held the silence.'

My son has also taught me two very valuable lessons about this technique:

- Avoid it for a repeating situation. My son kept getting frustrated with a particular piano piece he was learning. I'd been reflecting his frustration. Then one day he said, 'Don't keep telling me I'm frustrated, or it just becomes more frustrating.' Point taken.
- Also, don't let your kids know about the technique. My son over-heard me explaining it to another mum and months later told me that he knows when I've reflected an emotion and now holds the silence for ages to see what I'll do. OMG!

It's best to keep this technique for the special moments when they really need it. Use it occasionally and keep it subtle.

Get it right though and naming the emotion is like a key that unlocks people when they are overwhelmed. We then have to stay there, as solid steadfast Rock, while they unburden.

So, just to recap on reflecting the emotion:

- Avoid asking questions.
- Name the emotion.
- Use silence afterwards to enable the person to respond in their time.
- Remember less is more – use this technique sparingly when needed.

Warning: Don't use this technique if you are the cause of the speaker's emotional turmoil. If you cause me to feel anger, I don't want you to then tell me I'm angry!

when a question asks us to listen: reflecting a 'Do you...?'

Avoid the platitudes and the discomfort and reflect instead.

How many times have we all been caught on the back foot by a difficult question? As we discussed in Chapter 2, sometimes people will throw a 'do you' question at us to see how we might respond and I'm not sure they are always looking for our answer but rather permission to explore the subject with us, especially if they often repeat the theme of the question. It's like the speaker is really saying, 'Please can you support me as I explore this myself?'

So how to respond to a 'do you'? The best way I

have found is to reflect, but in a particular way. Rather than reflecting the actual question, we reflect our willingness to explore the subject raised by the question. Here's an example:

Speaker: 'Do you think I have a drink problem?'
Rock: 'Gosh… that's a really big question. Is that something you've been worrying about recently?'

Notice their Rock didn't dismiss, deflect, or respond with their opinion but simply reflected their willingness to hear more.

It depends on the context in which a statement like the one above was said – sometimes people will want you to say, 'No, of course not! You drink the same as me. It's fine.' But sometimes, a 'do you' is really asking:

'Can I open the door with you to this scary place in my head where I think I have a serious problem?'

By reflecting our willingness to listen we open the door to a conversation.

rock recap

Here's the reflection list:

- When words tell us what's wrong – reflect the drop.

- When emotions show us what's wrong – reflect the emotion.
- When 'do you' questions ask us to listen – reflect our willingness to be alongside.

The power of reflecting can be used in different situations to acknowledge someone's feelings and perhaps allow them to share. I started by practising reflecting with my family and friends to see what happened and how to get it right. It gave me confidence and it's utterly amazing to see it working.

Remember to keep any 'reflections' subtle. We can't make a drama out of it – it's much more delicate. It's being alongside the speaker rather than out in front.

There's no ego in listening.

Also, I intend to be 'Rock'. It might sound obvious but if a conversation suddenly changes from chit-chat and I become aware that the speaker wants to share their deep feelings with me, I mindfully say to myself 'Rock moment' to remind me to be present. And then I just listen and when they are done, they are done. I look out for the return. One word to watch for is 'anyway' as it indicates a change in conversational direction. My bestie has the most beautiful return: 'Anyway, that's enough about me. How's you?'

Listening binds the world together.

But to really be there for those around us we have to be aware of what makes us true Rock and it's the gift of empathy. I've become a big fan of the power of empathy and so we'll look at it more in Chapter 4 because I discovered that as much as I loved it, I wasn't always getting it right.

she can be a Rock because she too has been
in a hard place

4 empathy.

Trauma is not what happens to us, but what we hold inside in the absence of an empathetic witness. (Peter A Levine)

We now know to watch people's emotions, 'drops', and 'do yous', but I have discovered that there is another thing people do that can completely derail us. It's when someone just 'says it like it is', e.g.:

- My husband's having an affair.
- I've just been given a terminal diagnosis.
- I've been sacked from work.
- I'm being bullied.

We often struggle to reply to these statements because they are so big. It can be hard to know what to say or we worry about saying the wrong thing. Luckily, there is a way to respond ... and it's empathy.

'I sat with a middle-aged man who had been given a few weeks to live. He was understandably full of rage. He was so full of anger that he couldn't speak. I could have said, "you seem angry" but given the circumstances, I think that naming the emotion would have seemed very obvious and patronising. Instead I said gently, "I cannot imagine how you feel but it must be utter c**p". Then I sat quietly. He was quiet for a moment and then said, "No, it's not just c**p" it's … ."(I won't print the words here, but they weren't pretty!) When he had finished swearing, cursing, and ranting, he smiled at me and did the most beautiful return from a rant ever: "Do you want to hear about my life?" he said. "It's been utterly extraordinary. '"

So often empathy works best if it's reduced to a simple statement that just says, 'I get this must be hard' and acknowledges the impact of the situation. Also using swear words can really help but it does of course depend on who you are Rocking!

Empathy simply says, 'I can't possibly know how hard this thing is for you, but I can see that it must be hard,' in a few select words. And, if we can't find the words, empathy can be supportive silence.

'When someone shares something really big, I don't rush to respond verbally. Instead, I let them see me take a big breath in and a slow sigh out … It lets them know I've heard them and taken in the enormity of what they said.' (SJ)

Empathy might not always provoke a response. It might just be enough that they feel heard: that someone has acknowledged where they are and how difficult that place might be. In that moment, our empathy offers an open door to a future conversation and often that 'offer' is enough.

> We share with those who have earned the right to
> hear our story. (Brené Brown)

For the speaker, at the heart of being heard is trust: that we'll be there, accept their feelings, resist the urge to fix them, and definitely be the keeper of their secrets.

But sometimes I just wasn't rocking empathy.

getting it right

Empathy enables us to support someone in almost any situation (as we saw above), but I discovered that while I knew what empathy was, I didn't always know what it wasn't. I could define it but not always know how to use it.

Empathy is often described as the ability to share someone else's feelings or experiences by imagining what it would be like to be in that person's situation (i.e. walking in their shoes). But sometimes it can be hard to identify with someone's situation. How can we identify with someone whose football team loses the final when we don't care about football? How do you identify with a teenager whose boyfriend has dumped her when you've just been made redundant?

I learnt that the secret is this: don't empathise with

the situation; empathise with how their situation makes them feel. Focus on the emotion. For instance, we might not know what it feels like to watch a football team lose but we all will have experienced disappointment. We might think a teenager's love life is minor compared to losing our job, but we have both just experienced loss. So, it's our ability to access the feelings within ourselves that enables us to identify with another.

Empathy is identifying with someone's emotional response and affirming that it's okay for them to have that emotional response.

Three days after my mum died, a friend said to me, 'Oh, I know how you feel because my horse died last year.'

While I knew deep down what his horse had meant to him, at the time I wanted to scream: 'You have no idea how it feels because you still have your mum!' Of course, his only experience of grief might have been losing his horse, but by identifying with the comparison of our personal grief he caused me pain.

Thus, I've found that comparing stories can cause distress. Instead, it's recognising the shared experience of the emotion that can heal. It's better to say something that indicates that we understand someone's feelings. What if my friend, in the example above, had said instead, 'I too have felt grief. I know it can be tough. I'm here for you.'

No comparison: just empathy.

So, empathy works if we empathise with the emotions expressed rather than the narrative. Consequently, we must be cautious of equating an experience we've had with the one the speaker is sharing: to avoid the trap of saying, 'Oh, I know how you feel because ...' When someone is overwhelmed, they don't want to hear our stories; they want to share theirs. And even if our story seems very similar, we have to remember that our experience of it may be very different. Suppose two friends have both recovered from a similar illness. They share their recovery in common but how they are now feeling may be very different. Life may go on, but that life will be shaped by their personality, emotional resilience, support from family and friends, financial security, etc. I've learnt not to assume I know how someone is feeling.

Empathy is the shared experience of emotion rather than the story behind it.

I've also learnt that for empathy to be effective, I must follow it with silence: if I keep talking, I devalue my empathetic statement by not giving someone the space to feel my empathy. Turns out that a lot of the Rock magic is in the space we allow around our responses. And, of course, if I over-empathise, it's becoming about me and not the person I'm Rocking.

Sometimes people will choose us as their Rock

because they know we've had a similar experience. For instance, people tell me their 'grief' stories because they know I've 'been there'. Often people also seek my advice. It's such an honour to be part of those conversations, but I always remember to let the speaker 'lead' and share their story first.

the 'greet' mantra

If there is a mantra, I try to honour every day it's this one:

> Greet someone where they are and not where I want them to be.

We all have expectations of people – we want our partners, children, family, friends, and colleagues to be okay and behave in certain ways. But what if their behaviours don't match our preferences?

Let's look at some of my personal examples:

- When I desperately want to know how my son got on at his secondary school induction day but when I ask him what he did he just says, 'stuff'.
- When I want my friend to see how incredible she is but all she can do is compare herself to her sister.
- When I'm all menopausal and then hubby comes home cross about something, and I think, 'OMG get over yourself'.

- When my friend is too exhausted to see me, but I so need to see him?

Can we learn to accept another person's response even when it challenges us?

It can be hard to greet people where they are if it is directly opposite to how we feel. I guess we always have the choice: to argue and persuade them to our preference or to accept (and support) them 'where they are'.

'There is no getting away with people/children having feelings and we have to be alongside [them] when they are having feelings even if we find those feelings inconvenient.' (Philippa Perry)

Here's an everyday example (based on the memory of wanting a very skimpy nightshirt that said 'Every bunny's doing it' when I was 12!):

Mum: 'No you can't have that nightshirt – it's too grown up.'
Daughter: 'All my friends wear them. This is so unfair!'
Mum: 'Yeah well, life can be unfair.'
Daughter: storms off …

Or there's the 'greet':

Mum: 'No you can't have that nightshirt – it's too grown up.'
Daughter: 'All my friends wear them. This is so unfair!'

Mum: Stops what she is doing and becomes present and alongside her daughter. 'Yes, it must seem unfair. [note the reflection of the drop followed with silence]. 'It can be hard waiting to grow up [empathy].'

Sometimes I find it hard to understand or accept how someone is behaving. Indeed, it can be very frustrating when, for example, one friend is coping positively with a horrible situation and another friend is falling apart over what appears to be something fairly minor. But I try to remember that problems are always relative to the emotional strength and personal situation of the person facing them. Also, of course, I could be witnessing the tip of the iceberg – there could be a whole back story I just don't know about.

I've found that when I judge someone's behaviour or opinions, I'm more likely to dismiss their problem, disengage, or try the quick fix. But it turns out that we don't have to agree with them to Rock them!

'A joint friend was constantly being mean to me – making spiteful little comments. It got to the point where I didn't want to see her any more. I felt very low. My boyfriend tried to make it better – he pointed out her good points, made suggestions as to why she might be being difficult, even defended her. Result – I felt even worse. I began to feel that not only was she making my life horrible but now my boyfriend was on her team too. Then, one day, after a particularly challenging visit, as we waved her off in her car my boyfriend turned to me and

said, "It's nice waving goodbye to MOB isn't it?"
"What's MOB stand for?" I asked. He smiled.
"Miserable Old Bat-face!" In that moment the sun
came out. My man had greeted me where I WAS –
that she was being difficult and that I was
struggling. From then on things got better – we
could laugh about her behaviour and I felt
supported.' (Suzanna)

So, it turns out that empathy involves being
alongside someone whatever their situation and
their response to it. Get it right and someone feels
heard inside and out.

rock recap

Here's my empathy recap:

- Greet people where they are and not where
  we want them to be.
- Empathise with the impact of the situation:
  how their situation makes them feel. Focus
  on the emotion.
- Use a simple statement to convey you get
  what they're feeling or use touch or silence
  to convey you have really heard them.
- Avoid telling your story with the 'I know
  how you feel' statement.

However, it turns out that we all have something
that gets in the way of our empathy and our ability
to be epic Rocks. I call them 'the gremlins': our
default responses to a tricky situation.

watch out – I already have a response primed!

5 gremlins.

So, someone is telling me their problem and the first thing out of my mouth is my 'default' response! We all have them – the little gremlins that prevent us from listening and being present. I think mine will be with me for life but I'm learning to spot them and then ignore them.

Below are the things that instantly get in the way of Rocking and hence an empathic response. Most of them are 'default responses': what we immediately do or say in response to someone's difficulties. Sometimes, they will be appropriate – like instantly giving advice to our children. Other times, they really do get in the way of enabling someone to feel heard. Let's look at these inhibitors to being alongside.

fixing

Someone tells me their problem. Panic stations. I'll make it better: give them solutions. Quick, let's fix.

A trainee therapist visited a man in the last few

weeks of life. When she asked him if he wanted some company, he said, 'Not today as I'm writing my book ... not that I'll finish it.' He looked so terribly sad. The trainee was new and understandably panicked and felt she needed to respond – to make him feel better. She said, 'I'm sure you'll finish it; I can tell you're a fighter'. His response ... he asked her to leave.

Sometimes we just can't make things better. Rock is not something where we should feel the pressure to succeed. To 'be there' for someone is an immeasurable gift that can't be quantified and qualified.

Rocks don't run around looking for someone to fix; they are just a steady presence of support when needed.

To be fair, we do live in the ultimate fix-it society and a culture that believes that someone else always has the solution. So when we are faced with a friend in need, the temptation is to go into fix-it mode and start giving advice, suggest solutions, and worst of all, tell them why they shouldn't feel the way they do. I don't know about you, but when I have a problem, chances are I've already thought through all the alternatives, visited every possible solution, and constantly sh*t on myself about why I feel the way I do. So, I really don't want my friends to join in. What I need is their attention. I want to be heard because then I might feel worthy, empowered, justified, and validated. I might even sort out my head.

Fixing generally comes in two forms:

- We suggest lots of solutions.
- We quickly try to cheer them up.

But as we saw in the therapist example above – fixing doesn't necessarily help.

If ya really want to help can ya 'pause' being helpful?

Ever been rock climbing? The rock doesn't help us to climb – it supports us? It may sound a subtle difference, but I've learnt that if I'm in 'help mode' I'm assuming I have the answers and might disempower the person who needs to be heard. I try to remember that there is no right or wrong with feelings – they are just an emotional response to difficult times. If I aim to be supportive, I'm allowing those feelings to flow. I've realised that by inadvertently 'fixing' I can cause someone to repress their feelings. And we all know that over time repressed emotions can come out as anger, illness, depression, etc.

Also, I know (because I do it), when people are struggling, they often share their struggles with several people. But what happens if everyone is giving their ideas and advice? Sometimes well-meaning suggestions can change from being super useful to being overwhelming.

Be the one who listens first.

Sometimes other people's problems may feel minor compared to ours or others around us but it doesn't serve anyone to be reminded of that. Other times the situation can be very serious and it's hard to know what to say or we say too much.

Here some top tips to avoid the 'fixing fixation':

- Don't panic!
- I ask myself: 'Can I really make this person feel better by trying to fix this?'
- Observe myself whenever I do go into 'fix it' mode and see if it worked. Watch how I feel when someone tries to fix me.
- Greet them where they are – to remember that all problems are relative to the person experiencing them.
- Let go of judgement. Although, as Brené Brown says, this is hard 'especially when we all enjoy it as much as we do.'
- Trust. If I let them talk it through, they may find their own solution.

There will be times, particularly in a work setting or as parents that we will need to offer advice and solutions. My new mantra is this:

Rock before you Role!

If our role is to guide someone in the right direction, perhaps the best way to do this is to listen first so they feel heard (Rock) and then offer our advice (do our role).

When I'm in a dark place, please don't turn on the light. Instead sit in the darkness with me and let me be in charge of the light switch.

I've discovered that if we can greet people where they are (respecting their feelings and choices in that moment), we will support them as Mighty Rock Warriors. Try to fix them – and we become just another grain of sand in the many voices that speak to them without listening.

pity and sympathy

'Empathy is walking a mile in someone else's moccasins. Sympathy is being sorry their feet hurt.'
(R O'Donnell)

Many people ask me whether it's a good idea to be sympathetic to someone. I think we have to be careful because feeling sympathy, pity, concern, or sorrow for someone's situation is not the same as the ability to understand and relate to how they are feeling. And, as we know, being able to really relate to someone's situation is the bedrock of empathy.

- Sympathy and pity come from a place of feeling more secure and separate from the other person's situation.
- Empathy comes from a place of equality and togetherness: I might not be in your situation, but I too have had dark times and know what that feels like.

Empathy is being 'with them'; sympathy 'is being sorry for them'.

butting in

It's not just about being a listener – it's about letting the speaker be.

I try to avoid interjecting with the speaker's narrative. Questioning and interrupting are forms of taking control of the conversation and sometimes it just isn't helpful. Before I'm ever tempted to interject I ask myself why I feel drawn to do so.

One of the biggest reasons for our questions or interruptions is a genuine interest in what the person is saying or a desire to know what's wrong and help. However, true support is allowing someone to explore their own thoughts and solutions unhindered.

interrupting

Oh, I'm sorry – did the middle of my sentence interrupt the beginning of yours?

Interrupting is actually shorthand for 'listen to me because what I have to say is more important'. Interrupting breaks the flow of someone's speech or thought: the listener becomes the speaker and now leads the conversation. It's super frustrating when someone steals your voice.

'I get lost in people.' (Isla, aged 8)

However, I've noticed that sometimes the person who interrupts the most is the person in a group who feels the most unheard. Honestly, I do this a lot when I feel ignored or discounted, especially in groups. Observe those around you who interrupt – are they being rude or are they desperate to be heard too?

Sadly, interrupting completely damages connection and frustrates meaningful interaction.

questioning

Seriously?

Questioning is a great tool to elicit more information and guide someone to tell us what we need to know. However, in a Rock situation, it tends to be better to hold the questions and just let the words flow from the speaker. In other words, I don't question the person I'm Rocking; I question myself:

- Why do I feel the need to ask a question?
- What will be gained from hearing the answer?
- Can the question wait?
- What happens if I don't ask it?
- If I feel tempted to ask 'Why?' is it because I'm judging them?

While questions may direct the speaker; silence allows the speaker free reign to go where they want to go – and who knows where that will be or how that will bring relief. I'm learning to trust the process and watch the story unfold.

'When I have a problem, I wish my dad would stop asking me questions.' (Sam aged 13)

But let's be honest, this is the hardest gremlin to avoid – particularly as a parent. My gremlin is the, 'What's the matter?' question. I constantly upset my son by asking him what's wrong. I'm learning, slowly, to curb the inclination to make everything all right. My son told me that the questions make him feel more stressed. He said he'd just prefer a hug or some other simple response that shows I know he's upset and I'm there for him.

Oh, and top tip: we have to avoid asking questions with our eyes as well.

upstaging

Years ago, I am walking in town with my boyfriend and a man crosses the road in front of us. My boyfriend says, 'There goes Two Sheds'. 'Why do you call him Two Sheds?' I ask. 'Oh,' he says, 'cos if you have one shed, he has two!' So, from then on I've called it 'Two-shedding', when people steal the spotlight, upstage and boast gloat.

I have to be honest. I realised I did it. I discovered that when people shared an anecdote, I often had one to share too – only obviously mine was better! I would literally anecdote outshine them. It used to feel so good while I was doing it – but it never felt so good afterwards. I started observing myself and now (mostly) catch myself before I 'two-shed' someone. After all, do I really need more attention than they do? And wouldn't it be better if my friends think of me as a listener rather than someone who always has better stories.

I think there are two types of two-shedding or upstaging: light and dark. Light upstaging is when enthusiasm takes over and we push the speaker out of their joyful spotlight and take their place. Dark upstaging is 'You think you have it bad – listen to my story. My darkness is so much darker than yours.'

light upstaging

Light upstaging is when someone is sharing their good news and we upstage them. When someone is proud of something they've achieved, when someone has experienced unexpected bounty, when someone has overcome something they've been battling with, is it bragging to tell others or is it just joy being shared? We have all shared moments of pure happiness and there is nothing worse than someone trampling all over them.

'I was going to be interviewed on television. I was telling a friend about it. I was super excited. He asked me how long I was going to be on TV for. 'Oh about 5 minutes,' I said. My friend turned and smiled at me and said... 'Oh, I was on for 25.' My excitement balloon was well and truly popped!'
(Matt)

I've discovered the joy of no longer popping anyone's achievement/excitement bubble. Instead, I let them have their moment in the sunshine and watch them glow. It's actually much more fun.

Let them share their light.

dark upstaging

Dark upstaging is when we compete about how 'c**p' things are – it's like the worst possible game of Top Trumps.

Many times, other people's problems may feel minor compared to ours or others around us but it's still a problem to them. I find it so frustrating when people say things like, 'Oh you think you have it bad...' or, 'You should try living with...' because it totally devalues someone else's feelings.

> If I'm sharing a problem, I don't want to be upstaged by yours.

humour

> 'I don't know of anything that a bit of humour can't sort out.' (nurse) 'Yes, but sometimes things are too bad to laugh.' (elderly patient)

Humour can be a great 'lift' to someone facing huge difficulties and laughter can be a great healer. However, there will be times when it really doesn't work and is completely inappropriate. The secret is to be able to use humour when needed and not as a default response to a tricky situation.

at least

'At least' comments are a common default response and are often said to be reassuring. However, they can badly backfire and rarely work. Every time I teach Rock, I hear the pain that 'at least' comments have caused. It's one of the most destructive gremlins. I will share a few:

- After a woman miscarried: 'At least you had lots of presents.' (You can see why it doesn't work!)
- After someone's dad died: 'At least he was a good age.' (Not much of a consolation when you've just lost your dad.)
- After a child came second in a race, she had trained really hard for: 'At least you tried.' (Totally not recognising the obvious disappointment in the moment.)

escalators

And finally, there are the gremlin escalators – statements devoid of empathy that are guaranteed to escalate a situation or at the very least generate a negative response and usually a swear word or two. Here are some:

- 'Cheer up, it might never happen.'
- 'Poor you.'
- 'Do you have PMT?'
- 'Are you feeling better now?' (said with pity.)
- 'Nobody's dying.'
- 'Aren't you making a mountain out of a molehill?'
- 'Come on, buck up, pull yourself together, everything will be okay.'
- 'Why?'
- 'It's not my fault!' (when you aren't even blaming them)

Often gremlins arise because we feel uncomfortable and our default responses are then triggered. However, a great insight from a nurse has helped me. This is what she said:

> If you're feeling uncomfortable maybe you're actually picking up on how troubled the other person is.

Recognising this reminds me to lean into the discomfort and listen regardless.

rock recap

- Observe yourself whenever you are listening: what are your gremlins?
- Observe others: what are their gremlins?
- Knowing what gets in the way of your Rockness allows you to own your listening.

I try to:

fix it,

undermine it,

undervalue it,

ignore it,

avoid it,

upstage it,

lighten it

I reduce Rocks to rubble,

I am a Rock gremlin

On top of our 'gremlins' there are other things I've found that just get in the way. I call them the inhibitors …

no matter how hard I try to listen, sometimes stuff gets in the way

6 inhibitors.

As I began to embrace my 'Rockness', I realised there were lots of things that could totally derail me. Here's a few:

distractions

There are many outside distractions in life which make it hard to focus and listen: disruptions, interruptions, noise, being hungry or being tired. We can't plan for distractions – we can only do our best to be present in the moment.

However, watch out for the monster distraction gremlin – they come in many forms, but they always have a screen.

Modern proverb:

Man can't Rock and text at the same time!

ego

Icarusitis!

Remember the myth of Icarus who dared to fly too close to the sun: ego got the better of him. One of the most valuable lessons I've learnt from sitting with patients, is that here is no place for ego in being alongside. Rocks don't require anything of the speaker: they don't need thanks, praise, or gratitude, they are just happy being Rock. So, if we have thoughts like 'I'm going to Rock her and be amazing and change her life' let's slap ourselves.

Listening isn't a show it's a glow.

our body language

One thing I've learnt from observing myself (particularly as a parent) is that my body language can totally betray me. Like when your mouth says one thing and your body language is screaming something completely different. Turns out kids are epic at reading body language and they aren't fooled.

It's difficult to remain relaxed and open when we listen to something that challenges us. We may try to be non-judgemental but our body may reveal our true feelings.

Say something political or controversial to a group
of friends and watch everyone's body language
speak volumes.

Facial reactions, crossing our legs away from the
speaker, or folding our arms can give us away. And
trust me, the speaker will notice: they can read
body language too.

emotional reactions

A Rock does not participate with the flood of
emotions; a Rock is a safe place in a storm.

Part of our Rock life is hearing people's sadness:
tales of grief, loss, pain, loneliness, fear, and
vulnerability. It can be upsetting to hear these
stories. We can find ourselves welling up, feeling
hot under the arms, tears forming, or tightness in
our chest or throat. This is empathy: beautiful,
wonderful, amazing empathy.

Dacher Keltner, a psychologist at the University of
California at Berkeley, has discovered that we are
hard-wired for kindness. A part of our brain is
triggered when we experience empathy and this in
turn triggers our Vagus nerve. The Vagus nerve is
intimately related to how we connect with one
another – linking directly to nerves that tune our
ears to human speech, coordinate eye contact, and
regulate emotional expressions. So, when I feel my
body physically responding to someone's emotional

pain, I inwardly relax into it because that's what my body is supposed to do. Our bodies can empathise.

So, how then do we cope when we feel empathy but also need to keep our emotions in check?

I believe if someone is sharing something very painful with us and we shed a tear they will be touched by our empathetic response as long as it is authentic. Full-on blubbing, however, is obviously not the way to go. As an end-of-life companion, I've had many moments at the bedside when I can feel tears building; usually when others begin to cry. But my job is to stay Rock: a steady empathetic presence. My mantra is 'not mine'. I remind myself silently that this is not my grief but theirs. That I am a loving witness, but definitely a witness not a participant. It's not my story. Such reminders enable me to hold a steady presence for those who need my support. The secret is to remain empathetic, steady but also genuine.

us

One of the great inhibitors to our ability to Rock is us. We all come with our own baggage of self-limiting beliefs. And in my experience, nothing shines a light on our own weaknesses more than someone who appears strong where we are vulnerable. So, it can be hard to listen to someone if they are pressing our insecurity buttons.

Let's look at me. I am a mum, home-maker, and self-employed. My working life is what I call the 'Mumsy juggle act'. A good week for me is being there for my son and hubby and feeding them well, enjoying work without stress, and the house (and me) not looking too shabby. But I do have friends who seem to manage the impossible – they look beautiful, the house is pristine, they bake, they work, and they keep fit. I love them dearly and I wish I knew their secret. May be they never sleep!

Anyway, guess what would happen if one of these mums started telling me how great their day had been, how much they'd achieved, what a beautiful dinner and dessert they'd created? I might feel shame. I might not be able to greet them where they are (and let them share their joy) because of my own stuff. In order to own our 'Rockness' for others we have to look at our own emotional baggage or at least be aware of it. If we feel our own Rock gremlins rising when someone is talking to us, we need to breathe, acknowledge the gremlin, and put it in our back pocket. For now, we are Rock.

If you want to look at your stuff (my back pocket got pretty full), Brené Brown is a good place to start. The TED talk and following book *The Power of Vulnerability* are utterly epic. (Thanks, Brené – you totally Rock.)

I realised that my insecurities and feelings of shame would also provoke my competition gremlin. Competition is a great inhibitor to Rock because if someone presses our competition button it's hard to stay silent and attentive. Remember, we are most likely to react when someone is sharing their achievements in an area where we feel weak.

It only becomes challenging if it challenges us.

It helps me to remember that if it feels like someone is 'boasting' it could be that they are trying to justify stuff to themselves. When we feel vulnerable about life, some people self-deprecate, and some people do the exact opposite: they puff up. Sometimes 'look how great I am' can be code for 'I feel really insecure'.

it must be me

I love that bit in When Harry Met Sally (80s film – check it out if you've never seen it) where Harry keeps trying to call Sally. She doesn't pick up the phone and he leaves the following message:

'The fact that you're not answering leads me to believe you're either (a) not at home, (b) home but don't want to talk to me, or (c) home, desperately want to talk to me, but trapped under something heavy.' (When Harry Met Sally, 1989, Colombia Pictures)

I just love that because it's so not me! If someone doesn't return my call, my thoughts can run as follows:

'The fact that you're not answering leads me to believe you're either (a) upset with me, (b) upset with me, or (c) upset with me.'

In my head, if someone doesn't talk to me it's because I have done something wrong – not simply because they are busy, worried about something, etc. etc. If you, like me, suffer from 'Itmustbemeitis' there is a way out of the nightmare: changing the 'I must have done something wrong' to 'I wonder if something is wrong'. If we change the focus from 'us' to 'them' we might spot that something is wrong and become aware that they might need Rocking. We observe rather than react.

Using empathy works brilliantly here too. So the next time you're passing someone you know in the street and they don't make eye contact or look down or away, text them later with the ultimate empathy pebble: 'I passed you in the street today and you looked really preoccupied – hope things are okay. Love ya xx'. Then let it go and move on. The great thing too is that if, by some miracle, you have actually upset them, you've opened the door to a discussion.

insecurities

Being a Rock is about supporting someone else – so we can't let our 'worry' gremlins get in the way. Thoughts like

- Am I good enough?

- Can I do this?
- Will I remember everything they say to me?

just eat away at our ability to Rock.

It's also missing the point. Remember we don't have to do anything! We don't have to perform. We don't have to achieve. We don't even have to remember everything the speaker says. We aren't their counsellor; we are their Rock.

We need to soften into our own 'stable point' – the point where we feel steady, relaxed, and calm. Own our presence. There is a joy in this place – rest easy and just be.

> Just be you … it's all anyone ever needs.

when we get it wrong

> Don't beat yourself up; learn instead.

Sometimes we'll get it wrong. We will forget to stay present, observe, reflect, or stay silent. We will make mistakes. As much as we might intend to be there for someone, old patterns of behaviour can still butt in. The secret is to keep trying.

When I began to sit with people at end of life, I made loads of mistakes – well-meaning attempts to cheer them up and make them feel better. They were my teachers. They taught me that 'trying to do something' doesn't work; being alongside does. Sometimes we'll get it wrong – but when we get it right, it's amazing. If you make a mistake, pick yourself back up and start over. New skills take practice.

Mistakes are proof you are trying.

rock recap

- Be kind to yourself – sometimes life gets in the way of listening
- Be kind to yourself – sometimes 'you' get in the way of listening

But despite all these things, I've learnt that if I can, in the moment, rise above the distractions and my stuff, the joy of being alongside is waiting. The power of being Rock is subtle but its gift is huge. Through our presence, observation, reflection, and empathy people can feel truly 'seen, heard, and witnessed'.

Be an inspiring witness to everyone you meet (Pam Grout)

But it turns out, in order to listen to others, we also have to be heard. We also need Rock …

be heard too

PART 2.

ROCKING OURSELVES

Being Rock for others is a tremendous gift but sometimes it's our turn. We need to be heard! Turns out Rocking life is a two-way street: we can't be a Rock without being Rocked!

I've learnt, very much the hard way, that to seek Rock for ourselves we need to be brave, honest, and vulnerable. Yes, it takes self-care, but it also involves connection. We need to look after us and reach out to others.

So, let's look at how to Rock ourselves:

- How to spot we are approaching burn out: hearing ourselves.
- Self-care.
- Calling on our Rock crew and seeking the experts.

you have to be Rock to rock someone

7 hearing ourselves.

'A friend asked me to do some work for her – a freebie. It's the sort of thing I'd usually say, 'yes, of course' and do it. But I was low. Struggling. So I said, 'No, sorry, I can't'. And, for the first time ever, I felt proud of myself rather than guilty. I can value my own needs.' (Penny)

burnout

Years ago, I had a friend who constantly sought me out for emotional support. I was a Rock for her on many occasions. But then, when I needed her, I noticed she would 'disengage': sometimes very starkly by changing the subject or talking to someone else. Eventually I realised why: she couldn't be a Rock for me because she was too unstable herself. A few years ago, the same thing happened to me. Despite my passion for supporting people at the end of life, I found I couldn't cope with volunteering. I was struggling with depression and anxiety brought on by the menopause. Finally, I had to admit I couldn't be a Rock for myself let alone the people I encountered at the bedside.

But here's the funny thing, even though I was crying in front of the doctor, I didn't know I was in burnout. It's like I just couldn't see it. What I did know is I wanted to escape from everyone and everything because I felt so overwhelmed. I'd begun to put up barriers and was withdrawing.

Rock was becoming stone.

In hindsight I realise this was a huge warning sign. Turns out if we are putting up barriers to personal connection we are in burnout. Simply put, we are protecting ourselves – saving a bit of us for us.

All of us experience stress – it's the wear and tear of responding and reacting to life's pressures, demands, challenges, and changes. However, sometimes we become overwhelmed by cumulative stress – this isn't stress in the moment but rather a gradual and persistent build up. The trick is to spot that build up and seek help early on.

A chap called Maslach defined the stages of emotional burnout and I think they are super useful as a self-check. On a scale, if we are at 1 or 2 we need to switch to self-care mode. If we are at 3 or above, we definitely need to be reaching out for support.

The scale is:

- Feeling exhausted – turns out the body is smarter that the mind and responds

instantly to stress. We might feel tired but often can't sleep.
- Feelings of irritability and impatience.
- Cynicism and detachment – trying to save a piece of ourselves for ourselves.
- Physical complaints or depression (reactive to the situation rather than clinical).
- Disorientation and confusion.
- Feelings of being indispensable, e.g. I have to go to work, they need me.
- Minimisation and denial of feelings.

Knowing these has helped me keep track of 'me' but also spot warning signs with my family and friends.

All of us need to learn when and how to say 'no', because honestly if we can't support ourselves, we can't be there for others. It's so much harder to be a Rock when we have our own stuff going on. There are people we will always try to be there for: our children, partners, bestie mates, etc. But even then, it can be terribly hard to be present for someone if we are all over the place.

So how do we say 'no'? I learnt that I have to be honest with myself first and then honest with everyone else. Accepting my vulnerability and telling the hospice I needed a break was one of the hardest days of my life. How could I stop doing what I loved? I felt I was letting everyone down: the patients, the hospice, my fellow volunteers, and most of all me. I also had to tell my family and friends that I was struggling too – and ask them to understand that I was fragile and needed their support and understanding while I sorted myself out.

Put yourself first!

The truth is it is sometimes easier to be a Rock for others than for ourselves. How often do we give out without replenishing within? It has certainly been the case for me – in juggling the many aspects of my life, I forgot to nurture my core and be true to me.

To be honest, finding time for ourselves can seem impossible and I am definitely work in progress. Sometimes I keep on track, but when I'm busy it is easy to slip. I have to remind myself that self-care is my 'safety net'. I need to ensure I have top up 'me time'.

Replenish, rejuvenate, relax, restore

But what does 'me time' look like? At first, I thought it was finding time for a run, walk, coffee with a friend, etc. And while all those things restored me, they didn't last. I could be okay while I was doing those things, but then I would be stressed or down again once I was immersed in everyday 'busyness'. I realised I needed a plan: a format to support me. I realised I needed to learn to listen to my needs and be a Rock for myself. And then, the penny dropped – I could use the structure of PORE for me as well as others. Could presence, observation, reflection, and self-empathy support me? A new journey of discovery began.

presence

So, how to be present with myself? I knew that presence involves being alongside and the ability to be comfortable with silence. How, I wondered, could I apply that to me? I've never been particularly good at meditation – thoughts always get in my way – and yet I can hold presence for others; therefore there must be a key to holding presence for me. How?

Then I remembered what the people I sat with taught me, that presence has to be 'authentic'. So, expecting to turn myself into a yogic master and hold presence in silent bliss isn't realistic because it isn't me. However, sitting with a cup of tea and resting into the experience of it could be. Realising I'm not coping and taking some time out to breathe could be. Putting on my walking boots and knowing I need to be outside in the natural world could be.

Presence also involves silence. So, this is the point, right here, when I stopped writing this book. I realised I had absolutely no idea how to be silent with myself. In all of my experience of listening to others, I've sat in silence many times without any expectation of outcome. But had I ever, once in my life, sat in silence with myself without an agenda? Never! If I intended to be silent it had always been as part of a meditation or trying to be mindful. There it was again, 'trying' not 'being'. It was time to experience silence with anticipation not expectation.

I was home alone when I wrote this. I committed to 6 hours of silence – turned off the computer, the mobile, the radio, etc. Silence: just me, the cat, and the hamster. How hard could it be? Started off really easy – I enjoyed the sounds of cooking breakfast, stirring porridge – and then the 'thoughts' kicked in: 'Oh, look at you being mindful. See you do have an agenda. See silence can't be achieved without intention. You can't truly be.' [At this point you can insert a swear word of your choice. Said silently!]

Six hours later this is what I learnt. It's hard to be silent when you are connected to things – like when the cat tried to catch and eat a bee. I spoke. At least I saved the bee. But then something amazing happened. I heard my voice. Like really heard it and suddenly what I was searching for was there.

In order to hear myself, I don't have to be silent, I have to create silence. I have to give myself some space. I know it might sound obvious, and entirely ridiculous that I hadn't thought this through, but if I'm surrounded by noise, bustle, everyday living, guess what – I can't be present for myself.

So, presence requires a place of silence and allowing, even for a moment, stillness. Then breathe and just wait for my body and mind to calm. I need to envision my 'Rockness': steady, still, silent, and safe. Peace.

Create a presence space.

One of the hardest things that side-rails my presence, and I guess yours too, is other people: especially kids. I've come to realise that as a parent, even when I hide in the loo to breathe, he can be calling to me through the door. Also, if I'm home, presence is harder because I can spot things that need doing. It's hard to rest into silence and stillness when you notice the TV needs dusting.

So, I get out. I've found a tree. It's become, as Winnie the Pooh would say, my 'thoughtful' spot. The place I go to create some space and stillness so I can then become aware of me and greet myself where I am.

So, here's my presence checklist:

- Be honest – acknowledge you need to be a Rock for yourself.
- Find a still space.
- Be authentic – given the situation in the moment, don't try for perfect 'presence' but rather allow the presence you can achieve.

Okay, so far so good. But then I discovered there are 'presence' gremlins. These gremlins fool us into thinking that 'treating' ourselves to some time out is the same as being present. I discovered that there is a huge difference between presence and numbing.

Presence is time In; Numbing is time Out.

Numbing is a coping strategy I developed a long time ago. Rather than being present with myself in difficult times, I lost myself to my favourite escape strategy: alcohol. Many of us will be numbing without even realising it: disappearing into social media, gaming, Netflix, shopping, eating, drinking, etc., and it's not the same as being present with ourselves.

I've had to learn to spot the difference between 'presencing' and 'numbing':

- Presence is awareness. Presence allows us to be aware of ourselves: to experience the state of our being in the moment. When we are present with another, they become our focus. So, to be present for ourselves, we must become our focus.
- Numbing is distraction. It's the opposite of presence because instead of focussing on ourselves it totally diverts our attention. It's escapism. I can easily spend an hour on Twitter. I can immerse myself; switch my brain away from my worries. But the truth is, I've no more awareness of how I feel after 'Twitter time' than before it.

So 'numbland' doesn't work because while numbing blocks observation; presence allows observation. And we all know, we can't Rock without a bit of observation.

observing

You have to be present to practice presence.

So, I'm in my thoughtful space, resting against my tree and then I just softly observe: like I'm watching myself.

Here are some things I just bring my awareness to:

- Am I actually present?
- What's my body doing? Am I inner or outer? Is there tension in my body? Am I in fight or flight or am I slumped against the tree exhausted? Am I in physical pain?
- What's my brain doing? What am I thinking? Am I in a thought pattern loop? Is there a drop?
- What am I feeling? Can I name the emotion?

The trick is to just observe: to notice without any judgement. To accept ourselves as we are in the moment rather than where we expect or want to be.

reflecting

But is it possible to reflect for ourselves? I've discovered I can and what's more it enables me to take back some control. Here's a glimpse of one of my personal battles:

'Often, when I'm stressed or down, my thoughts take over and they can be overwhelming and uncontrollable. I call it 'TNTing'. TNT stands for 'toxic negative thinking' and it blows any presence I have to pieces. Once my thoughts take hold, I am in (what my neighbour calls) the spiral of s**t which just goes down and down. It's like being in a whirlpool from which I can't break free. Then one day I just reflected what I was doing. I just caught myself and called myself out: 'Oh, your TNTing!' And suddenly I was free from my destructive thought loop.'

Turns out that reflecting works because it switches us from being lost in the moment to taking back control. You can hear yourself! But how do we reflect for ourselves?

reflecting the emotion

What's the feeling?

The moment I identify an emotion (such as anger), I reflect it. But I've discovered it's really important how I reflect it. I say (out loud or in my head): 'This is anger' or 'I am feeling anger'. Reflection allows me to be aware of the emotion (e.g. 'anger') as something I'm experiencing rather than believing that it's something I am (i.e. that I am an angry person).

'When I had depression, someone told me to tell myself I was 'experiencing depression' rather than 'I was suffering from depression'. It left the window open to the possibility (albeit what felt like a tiny possibility at the time) that one day I wouldn't be depressed – that I would feel differently.' (Luke)

Also, once we've reflected the emotion, give voice to the thoughts and feelings that surface around that emotion. So, write them down, paint them, shout them out, sing them, rant in the shower, cry in the car. Whatever comes is perfect, but we've got to get them out.

For me, the best response to reflecting my emotions is to tell someone. I'm learning to call it out so I can then be Rocked.

'The car broke down. I was grumpy with my son. I said 'sorry' and then said, 'I'm feeling really stressed and cross.' Son's response: 'That's okay, Mum, I can see this is a stressful situation.' And do you know what? Suddenly it really wasn't stressful: suddenly it was me and my son and nothing else mattered.'

reflecting the drop

Do you hear your drops? Do you know them?

I have some common 'drop' themes. Knowing them has made the world of difference to me (and my hubby). My main one is: 'Every-where's a mess'. This is code for:

- I'm feeling totally overwhelmed with work/life/home commitments; or

- I'm menopausal – run now while you have the chance.

Hubby and I have learnt to acknowledge this drop together. So now the 'drop' is becoming our friend – it signals when I need some TLC and extra support.

If we learn to spot and reflect our own drops it really does help us cope and understand our feelings and needs: we become witnesses for our own self-care.

empathy

Be in your shoes and love yourself regardless.

But what if being present, observing and reflecting don't work, and we still feel like utter c**p? The answer – actually the only place to go – is empathy. We have to 'greet ourselves where we are'. Also, empathy requires us to be realistic and authentic. We need to find the courage to be honest with ourselves and allow our vulnerability.

But how do we give ourselves empathy? I was struggling with that until I met Philippe (an expert in non-violent communication). He taught me that behind every emotion there's a need; such as love, connection, friendship, security, etc. (see Maslow's 'Hierarchy of Needs' for a full list).

Understanding the 'need' underpinning the emotion changes everything: it allows us to be kinder to ourselves. Let's go back to my 'everywhere's a mess' drop. One of my biggest breakthroughs was discovering the need behind it. It's this:

Everywhere's a mess = I don't feel safe.

My parents' home had always been very clean and tidy, so while I love our 'homely' lifestyle, when I'm stressed, I seek the safety and security of an uncluttered house. Knowing that has changed everything because if I am feeling stressed, hubby and I now understand why the state of our home environment matters. The result – we tidy up first and then he hears me.

So, my best advice to empathise with yourself is to understand the *need* behind your feelings.

'I was acting like some demented woman the week before my son started secondary school.
Desperately trying to make sure he had everything and that everything was totally perfect (even the length of his shoelaces!).
I was driving myself mad.
Then I stopped and asked myself 'What's the need?'
It was simple: I wanted him to feel secure going into school.
Then I gave myself epic empathy – I turned nutter mother into epic mother just from hearing myself and how much I care and love him.'

gremlins

As we know from Rocking others, there is something that can derail empathy: those default responses or empathy gremlins. In terms of our personal self-care they can be:

- statements we heard as a kid (like 'pull your weight' and 'buck up')
- thinking we don't have time to devote to self-care
- feeling selfish
- worrying about what people will think if we say 'no', don't go to the party, put ourselves first, etc.

Watch out for the self-care gremlins and give to yourself.

Let's change the negative view 'giving in' to a positive 'giving In' – giving in to ourselves.

rock recap

So, here's the hearing ourselves list:

- Spot burnout (when Rock becomes stone).
- Give yourself some 'presence' space. Breathe.
- Observe without judgement.
- Reflect the emotion or spot the drop.
- Self-empathise.

So, once we know we need some 'us' time, what does self-care look like?

people don't burnout because they give too much; they burnout because they don't replenish

8 self-care.

For many of us self-care is one of the hardest nuts to crack. I can be utterly rubbish at it – especially when I'm stressed and need to care for me most. My main self-care gremlins are 'you haven't got time' and 'you're being selfish'. And those gremlins can be very vocal.

Self-care will be different for everyone, but we know it has to be authentic and we must make time for it. What's your self-care? What's the thing that always makes you feel better? (Remember it must make us feel better not just numb/distract us.)

Here's a list from my mates:

- swimming
- craft
- mad dancing in the living room when no one's watching (mine)
- massage
- jigsaw
- walking the dog
- down the pub with my best mate
- being in nature
- yoga

- book and beanbag
- climbing

The trick is to do something which totally relaxes your body and your mind. There is also lots of evidence that the natural environment is our best anti-stress gym. Studies are now showing how being in nature restores mental health. All of us need to 'rewild' regularly by spending time outside especially around trees. Scientists are now proving the healing effect of trees. Trees release essential oils called phytoncides which actually improve human immune systems. Studies of twenty-year olds in Japan found that forest visits lowered their cortisol, pulse rates, and blood pressure.

So, doses of nature are recommended for all of us, especially if we live in urban environments and much of our lives are spent interacting with screens. We need to get outside in nature, turn off our phones and Fitbits and just wander.

Don't effort; just be alongside nature.

The other way to reboot is to do a physical activity which engages your brain as well as your body. Dance and rock climbing, for instance, require our brains to focus on the activity and away from anxiety.

The secret I found is to make time commitments to 'being me' and stick to them. I found the way to achieve this was not to let my thoughts derail me with 'but you have so much to do', 'do it later', 'you can skip it today and spend more time on it tomorrow'. Instead, each day I commit some time to me. Now, when I do slip up, I genuinely miss 'my time' – so something has changed.

There is one other awareness that has helped me, more than anything, focus my self-care (thanks to Neale Donald Walsh for this one). I call it knowing what my life's dance is. All we have to do is figure out the answer to this question:

I am happiest when I'm being …

Just fill in the dots. It took me a week to nail mine. Remember it's asking, what are we happiest 'being' not 'doing'. Here's mine, in the hope that it helps you find yours:

I am happiest when I'm being inspired and being inspiring.

It has helped me realise that it doesn't matter what I do as long as I'm being inspired by someone, a book, an action, a project or that I am, in turn, inspiring others in whatever way I can. So now, when I get low, I seek a bit of inspiration. And when I'm on a high, I try to pay it forward.

rock recap

Self-care list:

- What's your self-care?
- Make time for you.
- Rewild.
- What's your life's dance?

So now I am learning to be a Rock for me. However, to be heard, sometimes we'll need our Rock crew and require the connection to others.

we all need connection …

who's in your Rock pool?

9 being heard.

Every listener needs to be heard.

Every observer needs to be seen.

Every Rock needs a Rock.

While being a Rock for yourself is a fantastic resource (you always have you with you), sometimes we just need another to hear us. Sometimes being heard by our Rock crew of friends and family will be enough; other times we'll also need the experts.

rock crew

Having support from those around us is essential. It's our connection with others that allows us to feel seen, heard, and witnessed.

Of course, not everyone can be Rock for us in every situation. We need to choose our people. Our circle of family and friends will include those who can hear us when we are sad and those who can hear our joy. There will be others who don't really fall into the listener category, but they might be the person of choice for work advice, a good laugh down the pub or a weekend away sharing a hobby. Then there are those friends are epic at helping practically in hard times by looking after the kids, etc. (these are our 'doing' Rocks). The secret is to not expect everyone to be everything. We need to value our Rocks for the gifts that they have.

When I lost myself to depression, I knew I needed my Rock crew. So I made a list of the people in my life I could go to for the following:

- Having a laugh with.
- Talking over work.
- Talking relationships or parenting with.
- Sharing hobbies.
- Sharing beliefs.
- My 'whoop whoopers'! My parents were brilliant at saying well done if I achieved something and genuinely being pleased for me. But I've noticed that some people find it hard to be enthusiastically supportive of others. So, if we have people in our lives that uplift us, who are proud of us and our achievements, we must keep them.
- The ones who know the 'real' me (like my mate Pete who still sees the 20-something girl behind the 50-something me – love him for that!)
- The doers – the one's I could rely on for practical support.
- Finally, there are the people who can really

Rock: the ones who hear our pain and joy without butting in – the people who get us and love us no matter what. These are our Mountains – our epic Rock people!

What I discovered in making my list is that several people appeared more than once – and some of those friends I don't see so often because they live a bit too far away. So now I know how important they are to me, I have made a pact with myself to see more of my crew.

extra support

You are only as sad as your secrets.

If you dear reader are struggling, please tell someone. And if it's too big for everyday support, please seek professional help. Remember you can choose your expert – so search for someone who makes you feel at ease. If you are with a counsellor, psychotherapist, or psychologist who just doesn't seem the right fit, don't give up. There is someone out there for you.

'I was referred to a psychiatrist. She sat behind a huge mahogany desk and looked very imposing. It didn't work for me. Weeks later I went to see a counsellor in her bungalow. We sat together in her living room and had tea and biscuits. She put me at ease. She turned my life around.' (Fern)

At the end of this book is a list of Helplines if you need support right now. Reach out – you are so worth it. I've called the Samaritans three times in my life – they listened and offered the support I needed. The last call I made paved the way to turning my life around.

As I write this, I'm showing signs of burnout. I can 'talk the talk' but have neglected my self-care – given out without 'Giving In'. Luckily, I have an epic Rock neighbour who gently pointed out that I need to reach out for some TLC. (Thanks, Jen)

rock recap

For self-support, here's the list:

- Be. Be present with yourself. If you feel happy, sad, frustrated, angry, just stop, be Rock for yourself, and notice it.
- Be honest. You can't hear yourself without being authentic. Don't feel that you should feel something – accept the something you feel.
- Be an observer. Do not judge yourself. Try not to analyse. Just observe.
- Be reflective. What emotion are you experiencing? What's your drop?
- Be still. Now rest. Be silent. Give your body time to realign to your refreshed self.
- Be home. Come home to yourself: back to your normal life. Stamp your feet, make a cuppa, come back to you.

- Reconsider. Are you okay or do you need to do more self-care, speak to someone from your Rock crew or reach out for professional support?
- Remember you are worth everything. You deserve to be heard.

Life is a complex mix of situations and experience. Every day you have endless thoughts and emotions. But you are Rock, while waves of emotions and thoughts may buffer you, weather you and change you, at your core, deep down within, is the pure you. And your Rock presence is your gift to you and the world.

You know you're getting it right when you're in a café and your nine-year-old says, 'Hey, Mum, that lady over there is Rocking her friend'.

and finally.

As I began to integrate Rock into my life, I began to notice some important things about living it.

being a diamond

> The best Rocks have a diamond centre – you don't have to see it to know it's there.

Not every moment of difficulty is a Rock moment. Sometimes when life is overwhelming, we can't even begin to find the words to share. We are so 'full up' we can't speak. Other times, we need to distract ourselves from the situation because right now we can't even process it or face it. That's when we need a 'Diamond' rather than a Rock.

The Diamond is the one who takes us down the pub to talk about football, takes us clothes shopping, bakes us cakes, and just chats to us about anything else over endless cups of tea. The role is to help us escape. Sometimes we all need a bit of love and distraction until we are strong enough to face our demons.

'I couldn't talk about what I was going through. But I loved hearing my son talk about my granddaughter's party. Sometimes it's nice not to think about your own problems.' (Linda)

Other times we can't continue a conversation because of the environment and proximity of other people. Learn when to be Rock and when to be a Diamond. If the speaker suddenly wells up, looks embarrassed, and shakes their head, they are indicating they can't share any more right now.

'I was listening to a colleague at work. She had been feeling low and I was validating her feelings with some empathy. Suddenly she welled-up with tears and looked embarrassed. I switched tack [to Diamond mode] and said with a smile "Anyway, I'll shut up now."' (Simon)

moving forward

When we get better at 'Rocking' we begin to notice those who find being a Rock trickier. This can bring its own challenges. What happens if we spend lots of time supporting different friends but when we are low, they aren't there for us? It's worth remembering that we all can respond to another's difficulties with suggestions, platitudes and stock phrases because that's what we've learnt to do. I'm sure we've all been hurt and hurt others with a well-meant comment. Noticing when someone doesn't support us can be frustrating but it's also really good news – it means we've changed.

You have to be Rock to notice who isn't.

As we move forward, we will spot cases of non-Rock from our friends, colleagues, and loved ones. I love the quote from Mahatma Ghandi:

Be the change you want to see.

It's a good mantra to live by. By being Rock for others we might just inspire them to listen more. We will witness many Rock errors – in ourselves and others. The secret is to keep improving ourselves and lead the way.

rock (r)evolution!

Thank you for the times you have enabled people to feel heard and for the Rock moments you will create in the future.

Rock people are 'uplifters' – through their steady presence and authenticity they uplift those around them.

I believe if we inspire others to Rock, then together we will create mountains of support.

We may never fully know the impact of a moment of being alongside someone. But just as ripples swell out from a pebble cast in a pool, I believe empathy and listening magnify outwards and positively affect the lives of everyone around us.

We don't talk; we listen.

We don't question; we observe.

We don't judge; we reflect.

We don't react; we support.

We don't compete; we empathise.

You Rock!

Sometimes, when you listen to someone as they pour out their heart, you will have the ultimate experience of being Rock. It's utterly amazing – and you will know it when you've done it. It's when time stops. It's as if you're both in a bubble: you watch as someone resolves deep hurts while you gently guide or choreograph them with your presence, attentive body language, and the rare reflection. And in this place, miracles occur. People release, share, resolve, laugh, cry, and find hope – all through you.

Practice whenever you can. Remember, words allow you to understand something, but experience allows you to know it. Honour your Rockness and share your gift by being there for others and yourself.

Feel free to send me your Rock moments to inspire me and others. I will share them on social media so others can be inspired by you. Just contact me at www.mandypreece.uk or @mandyjpreece

Also, if you have enjoyed this book, I would be eternally grateful if you could tell your friends or leave a review on Amazon.

Here's to being Rock ...

The greatest honour of my life has been to listen: to
hear the stories of wonder and the tales of grief
and through them see people surrender to their
feelings and finally unburden.

acknowledgements.

I've always been blessed with family and friends who have made and do make all the difference to my life. Thank you everyone. However, there is one friend who deserves a special mention, when I was at my lowest point and the only solution was alcohol, it was the loving words from Julie Charalambides that turned my life around. Now 19 years sober I can put into print what a gift she gave me.

Thanks to my particular Rock crew – you know who you are, and I love you!

Huge chi to Clara Apollo of Conscious Living Events both for her Foreword and her inspiration in my life and the lives of many. Massive thanks to Katherine Parker of Delightful Design for my branding and beautiful book cover and constant insight and support – I love working with you! Big hugs to Diane Page of Critical Publishing for her wisdom and guidance and general all round Rockness. To Jenny Berry for her inspired support and Debbie Butler, Mary Carruthers, Claire Cox, Alexis Mack and Fi Mackeith for reading the first drafts and their insightful comments.

Thanks to Pete of PreWeb It Solutions for keeping my website going and helping me traverse the intricacies of being online and to Emma Mitchell for taking the manuscript towards published reality.

Much love to Felicity Warner who embarked me on this incredible journey and Anita Rigler who supported and championed my volunteer journey. And of course, deep gratitude to all the remarkable people I sat with at the end of their lives who taught me the gift of being alongside and gave me so much of their wisdom.

And finally, thanks to my darling hubby, my mountain Rock, confidant, best friend, and fellow explorer of ideas. You Rock, Simon Curson, and I love you.

And then there's Arun – the best surprise anyone could ask for. Loves ya!

helplines.

The helpline numbers are for anyone who needs urgent support or feels at risk of suicide. The worldwide list accessed from the link below will provide more in-depth information for all the main support available wherever you live.

Australia
Crisis support service Lifeline is 13 11 14 (24 hours)
Canada
1-833.456.4566 (24 hours)
UK
YoungMinds Crisis Messenger: text YM to 85258 (free 24/7 support)
Samaritans: 116 123 (24 hours)
Mind: 0300 123 3393; text: 86463 (work hours)
Hopelink (if you are a young person at risk or are worried about a young person at risk of suicide): 0800 068 41 41
US
National Suicide Prevention Lifeline 1-800-273-8255 (24 hrs)
Worldwide
For a full list worldwide, please see:
https://en.wikipedia.org/wiki/List_of_suicide_crisis_lines

Printed in Great Britain
by Amazon